SADLIE
FAITH A
WITNE

A Course on
Catholic Belief

Journal

Sr. Helen Hemmer, I.H.M.

William H. Sadlier, Inc.
9 Pine Street
New York, NY 10005-1002

Nihil Obstat
✠ Most Reverend George O. Wirz
Censor Librorum

Imprimatur
✠ Most Reverend William H. Bullock
Bishop of Madison
June 16, 1997

The *Nihil Obstat* and *Imprimatur* are official declaration that a book or pamphlet
is free of doctrinal or moral error. No implication is contained therein that
those who have granted the *Nihil Obstat* and *Imprimatur* agree with the
contents, opinions, or statements expressed.

 is a registered trademark of William H. Sadlier, Inc.

Home Office:
9 Pine Street
New York, NY 10005–1002

ISBN: 0-8215-5632-0
3456789/98

Contents

CHAPTER 1

The Amazing Search for God

The desire for God is written in the human heart.

Reflection

It is truly amazing to me, God, to know that you planted this desire for you in my heart even before I was born. You must really want me to know you!

My prayer:

Loving God, I thank you for this very precious gift.
Help me to use it well. I pray that I will

. . . .

The search for God is part of being human.

I never really thought about this connection before. And yet
I can see evidence all around me that many people are searching
for you, God. I am glad to know that I am not alone in my search.
I am coming to realize

No matter where I go, I find the influence of religion.

From Stonehenge to the magnificent cathedrals and places of worship today, I can see the influence of religion. The desire to honor you, God, is alive and well.

Keeping my desire for you alive and well is important to me, God. This year I especially want to

. . . .

The practice of religion is universal. It is found all over the world.

From the beginning of time, human beings have marveled at the heavens. They even gave names to the sun, the moon, and the stars. They were searching for you, God.

My prayer:
You are greater than the sun and the moon and the stars.
You are greater than all creation.
When I look up to the heavens I want to say to you, God,

God, help me to grow in my desire for you.

CATHOLIC ID

Pope John Paul II recently wrote this about people of other religions: "Christ came into the world for all these people. He redeemed them all and has His own ways of reaching each of them."

Lord Jesus, teach me your ways.

You came into the world for all people
including those of other religions.
Help me to be as accepting of them as you are
and to

. . . .

We all need reminders!

The very names of the planets, the months of the year, and even our space rockets should be reminders of your presence, God.

Am I a reminder to others of your presence?
I try to be when I

Abraham

risked everything to follow God's invitation.

Reflection

You have called me, God, as you did Abraham long ago. You want me to follow you. This is a big challenge for me today. I know it involves risks.

Please give me the courage to take the risks that come with following you.
Help me to

........Journaling Notes ....

Use this space for any other thoughts you might have.

God, help me to grow in my desire for you.

CHAPTER 2

A Divine and Awesome Invitation

The most important things we know about God come from God himself.

Getting to know someone just doesn't happen by chance. It takes time, and it takes desire to know another person. God didn't leave anything to chance. He has opened himself to us and has let us know his deepest self. This is truly amazing! Just imagine! God wants me to know him!

What about me? Have I left my coming to know you, God, to chance? I hope not. When I think about it, I

You have invited me into a deep and personal relationship with you, God. How awesome! An invitation from God!
The more I learn about this invitation, the more I

Revelation always happens between God and people.

God making himself known to us is called divine revelation.

> "In times past, God spoke in partial and various ways
> to our ancestors through the prophets;
> in these last days, he spoke to us through a son."
>
> *Hebrews 1:1–2*

Revelation is much more than meets the eye. It is full of mystery. I may not understand it completely, but I know I experience God's presence in my life. I can say this because

My prayer:
I ask you, Lord Jesus, to fill me with a great desire to come to know and to believe in all that God has revealed. Help me to

In Jesus, God has told us everything we need to hear.

God not only revealed himself but made sure his revelation would be passed on from generation to generation.

"The apostles received the gospel for us from the Lord Jesus Christ; and Jesus Christ was sent forth from God. Christ, in other words, comes with a message from God, and the apostles with a message from Christ."

Saint Clement of Rome

What am I doing to make sure this message of Jesus is passed on to other generations? How well do I know the message? Is this something I really care about?
Right now I would have to say

Sacred Scripture is the written record of God's revelation to us. When I read Scripture, I

My prayer:
Jesus, you have so much to tell me. Give me a great desire to spend time with you in prayer and to

The truths of revelation are given to us in the deposit of faith.

The deposit of faith is a living thing, a dynamic treasure to be proclaimed and lived in every age.

> *"Guard this rich trust with the help of the holy Spirit. . . ."*
>
> 2 Timothy 1:14

My prayer:

Help me, Lord, to remember that you have entrusted this rich treasure to me. Help me to keep this precious gift alive in my heart by

. . . . Journaling Notes . . . .

Use this space for any other thoughts you might have.

In Jesus, God has told us everything we need to hear.

CHAPTER 3

Divine Gift and Human Response

Faith is a supernatural gift from God.

The search for truth begins in the heart of a believer.
When I look into my heart, I find a precious gift
from you, God, with the name FAITH on it.
It excites me to know that you have
given me the gift of faith. What a treasure!

I want to thank you, God, and tell you that

. . . .

Faith is something living.
It needs to be nourished and allowed to grow.

You know, God, that my faith is important to me.
I know I can do more to help it grow and to strengthen it by

"For by grace you have been saved through faith, and this is not from you; it is the gift of God."
Ephesians 2:8

Faith is gift. Grace is gift.
Gifts are given for a reason.

Gifts are given as signs of love and with the expectation that they will be accepted, cherished, and used.

My prayer:
Loving God, do you hear me saying loud and clear, I accept!
I accept your gifts of faith and grace.
Hear my prayer that I will

CAUTION
Actions speak louder than words.
It is easier said than done.

I know what these slogans are saying.
Giving witness to my faith is not always
going to be easy, but I

13

faith is the basis of our personal relationship with God.

A Lifelong Challenge

Exploring our faith is a lifetime project.

Faith is all about my relationship with you, God. Relationships grow and change every day.

You make a difference in my life everyday, and that is important to me.

This is where I think my relationship with you is right now:

Resolution:

On the ———— day, in the year of our Lord, ————————

I, ———————————————————————— , resolve to make

exploring my faith a lifetime project.

With the help of God's grace and my earnest desire to cooperate with it, I make this resolution freely and with confidence that I can accomplish it.

> *"Do not let your hearts be troubled.*
> *You have faith in God;*
> *have faith also in me."*
>
> *John 14:1*

My prayer:

When my heart is troubled, God, help me to remember that

. . . . Journaling Notes . . . .

Use this space for any other thoughts you might have.

Faith is the basis of our personal relationship with God.

CHAPTER 4

The God Who Reveals

We begin to know someone when
we know that person's name.

Reflection

I know your name, God.
Your name is YAHWEH, and it means "I am who am."
But I want to know more than your name.
I want to know

> *"Fear not, for I have redeemed you;*
> *I have called you by name: you are mine."*
>
> Isaiah 43:1

You make it very clear to me, God.
You know my name!
You have called me by my name.

Who would ever have guessed?
We know each other's name!
This makes me

My prayer:

Lord God, you hear me call you by many different names.
But my favorite name for you is
this is because

God, you created by your word. You spoke, and everything came into being.

Creation is God's first word to us.
Creation is a word?
When I think of it, creation does speak to me.
It tells me things I can't know any other way.

God, my creator, tune me in to the word that
you speak to me through creation.
Give me a listening heart so that I

**Some things in creation that speak
to me in a special way are**

*Fools say in their hearts,
"There is no God."*

Psalm 14:1

When I look into my heart, I know you exist, God.
I'm no fool. I find you everywhere, especially when I

God always was and always will be.

ETERNAL
ETERNAL
ALMIGHTY
ALMIGHTY
ALL-KNOWING
ALL-KNOWING
ALL-PRESENT
ALL-PRESENT

Reflection

These are powerful words used to describe you, God.
And yet, I believe that you are more than all these words together.
You are truly awesome!

When I think about you, God, and talk with you,
these are the words I like to use:

So Many Ideas about you, God, come into my mind now.
Be with me as I try to write them here in my journal.

Quietly pray this prayer of a famous monk:

> *Write your blessed name, O Lord,*
> *Upon my heart,*
> *There to remain so indelibly engraved,*
> *That no prosperity, no adversity*
> *Shall ever move me from your love.*
>
> Thomas à Kempis

Some thoughts on what this prayer means to me:

. . . . Journaling Notes . . . .

Use this space for any other thoughts you might have.

God always was and always will be.

CHAPTER 5

The God Who Is

Holiness is the essential characteristic of God.

> Holy, holy, holy is the LORD of hosts!...
> All the earth is filled with his glory!
>
> *Isaiah 6:3*

Reflection

These are familiar words to me. I hear them at Mass.
I wonder if I ever really think about what they are saying.
Do I make them my prayer of praise and adoration to you God?

My prayer:

All-loving God, I want to honor you not only with words but also with

God alone is holy.
God is the source
of all holiness.

My prayer:

Loving God, I like the idea of my prayers as incense before you.
This image reminds me that

> For what great nation is there that has gods so close
> to it as the LORD, our God, is to us whenever
> we call upon him?
>
> Deuteronomy 4:7

I know that you are close to me, God. But I also know that I need to be reminded of your closeness. Some things that do this for me are

God, if someone asked me who you are to me, do you know what I would tell them?
I would say

CATHOLIC TEACHINGS

The Church teaches that all during life we are surrounded by the watchful care and intercession of the angels.

Angels are popular today.
From books to TV programs,
to angel pins and prayer cards—
you name it!

Just Imagine!

Angels watch over me! They intercede for me!

My prayer:

There is only one God, who is the Blessed Trinity.

The Blessed Trinity is the central mystery of the Church.

 A mystery is a truth of faith that we know only because God has revealed it to us.

It is the work of believers to **Pray**, **Study**, and **Grow in Understanding** of the mysteries of faith as much as they can.

This is my challenge.
My resolve:

Probably one of the first prayers I ever learned was the sign of the cross. I am only now coming to realize how significant it is to my Catholic faith. How can such a simple prayer be so powerful!

My prayer:
God, help me to believe in you and honor you as Father, Son, and Spirit. Let the sign of the cross be a reminder to me that

*T*hrough him,
with him,
in him,
in the unity of the Holy Spirit,
all glory and honor is yours,
almighty Father,
for ever and ever.

To this prayer I say, Amen!

My Amen means that I

·········Journaling Notes·········
Use this space for any other thoughts you might have.

There is only one God, who is the Blessed Trinity.

CHAPTER 6

An Unfinished Image

> *God created man in his image;*
> *in the divine image he created him;*
> *male and female he created them.*
>
> *Genesis 1:27*

Reflection

God, some things make me wonder. For one thing, you created me in your image and likeness. You gave me an immortal soul! How good can it get! You must really love me.

My prayer:

How can I ever thank you, God, for all you have given me. I want you to know

In His Image

. . . .

I know I have a choice to make: either to grow in the image and likeness of God or to remain an unfinished image.

I can't imagine myself staying an unfinished image. What a thought!

Dear God,
I know what I have to do. It comes down to

> *God looked at everything he had made,*
> *and he found it very good.*
>
> *Genesis 1:31*

God, you created me good.
This is really important for me to remember.
When I look at myself, do I see a good person?

Loving God, how do you see me?

GRATEFULNESS

Reflection

It is hard to imagine anyone being ungrateful for such wonderful gifts
as eternal happiness and a personal relationship with you, God.
But that's what happened.
Ungratefulness is one of the reasons sin and evil came into the world.

Where do I stand when it comes to being grateful to you, God,
for the many gifts you have given me?

In all honesty, I would have to say

My prayer:

I am created in the image and likeness of God.

What a powerful picture!
I wonder why people wanted an image of Christ looking down
on their city?
They probably

If I were able to carve an image of Christ, what would it look like?
What would I want it to "say" to people?

*W*hat a marvelous creature a human being is that God
would even think to become one of us at the incarnation!

Jesus, you became one of us. You know our struggles.
Hear my prayer:

. . . . Journaling Notes . . . .
Use this space for any other thoughts you might have.

I am created in the image and likeness of God.

CHAPTER 7

The Perfect Image

When the fullness of the time had come,
God sent his son, born of a woman.

Galatians 4:4

This is a picture of Jesus' hometown today.
He really did live here on earth. He became one of us.
He had many of the same experiences that I am going
through now.

My prayer:
Jesus, it means a lot to me to know that you understand
what it is to experience the ups and downs of life. I need
your help today to

Mystery

What a great mystery: Jesus Christ is both God and Man.
I know a mystery calls for faith, for belief.
This is what I believe about you, Jesus:

> *You are my beloved Son; with you I am well pleased.*
>
> Mark 1:11

Jesus pleased the Father in everything he said and did.

BELOVED Dear God, I am "beloved" to you, too!
You created me in your image and likeness.
You are my God, and I am your child.
For such a great blessing, I want to say

PLEASED Dear God, I want you to be well pleased
with me in everything I say and do.
Are you pleased with me now?
When I think about this, I

My prayer:
God, it is important for me to know that I am beloved and that I can please you. Help me to respond to this love you have for me. Help me to please you by

Jesus is truly divine and truly human.

The gospel accounts are mainly concerned with what Jesus DID and what he SAID.

Reflection

I have learned many wonderful things about you from the gospels, Jesus. One thing in particular is that we, too, are to bring God's love to others just as you did.

You visited the sick and suffering.

I did this when I

You showed compassion to others.

I did this when I

You told others about God's love for us.

I did this when I

You reached out to the poor and lonely.

I did this when I

My prayer: Jesus, I have tried to reach out to others just as you did. It is not always easy to do, is it? Please be with me and help me to

> *Jesus advanced in wisdom and age and favor*
> *before God and man.*
>
> Luke 2:52

Reflection:

> Jesus, you had to grow in knowledge just as we do.
> You didn't have automatic answers to life's problems.
> You even had to learn how to pray.
> I find this really encouraging.

My prayer:

. . . . **Journaling Notes** . . . .

Use this space for any other thoughts you might have.

Jesus is truly divine and truly human.

CHAPTER 8

Messiah, Lord, and Savior

> Do not be afraid; for behold, I proclaim to you
> good news of great joy that will be for all the people.
> For today in the city of David a savior has been born
> for you who is Messiah and Lord.
>
> Luke 2:10–11

Good News

Jesus is Messiah.
The good news about this is

Jesus is Lord.
The good news about this is

Jesus is Savior.
The good news about this is

Mission Accomplished!

Jesus, you fulfilled your mission. You brought salvation to the whole world. You restored our friendship with God. You are our Savior!

My prayer:
Lord Jesus, thank you for being my Savior.
I have a mission in life, too. Help me to

> *Blessed are those who hear the word of God and observe it.*
>
> Luke 11:28

These words, Lord, challenge me to

> It's not just
> the **HEARING**
> that matters.
> It's the **DOING**
> that makes the
> difference.

Reflection

Jesus, I marvel at the many miracles you worked.
You raised the dead; you gave sight to the blind;
you cured lepers and even calmed the seas.
No wonder people called you the "miracle worker"!

My prayer:

Your miracles really make me wonder, Jesus.
But even more, I wonder at your great love for me.
In my heart, I know I love you, and I do try
to listen to your word.

Please hear my prayer that I

Jesus Christ is our Savior.

> *No one has greater love than this,*
> *to lay down one's life for one's friends.*
>
> John 15:13

No Greater Love

You gave your life for me, Jesus.
There is no greater love than this.
Your sacrifice lives on today primarily in the sacrifice of the Mass.
Do I believe this?
Does the Mass mean more to me than just time in church?

Hear my prayer, O Lord, that

Lamb of God,
you take away the sins of the world,
have mercy on us.

My prayer:
Lamb of God, you take away my sins.
Lamb of God, have mercy on me.
Lamb of God,

Lord, by your cross and resurrection
you have set us free.
You are the Savior of the world.

Lord, I believe you are my Savior.
I believe you have set me free.
I pray that I

.........Journaling Notes.........

Use this space for any other thoughts you might have.

Jesus Christ is our Savior.

CHAPTER 9

The Good News of Jesus Christ

*The Paschal Mystery:
The passion, death, resurrection
and ascension of Christ*

My Lord and my God!
You did all this for me!
I am loved by you.
Help me to believe this with all my heart.
Give me a strong faith so that I

Reflection

Your resurrection, Jesus, astonished your followers and challenged their faith to the limit. For them such a happening was hard to believe. Even your disciple, Thomas, who experienced so many of your miracles, needed proof before he could believe. It's not always easy to believe.

My prayer:

Risen Christ, I believe in you.
I know my faith has to grow.
Sometimes I am like Thomas.
When I find it hard to believe,

Trust God because God cares. [1]

> *Do not worry and say, "What are we to eat?" or*
> *"What are we to drink?" or "What are we to wear?"*
> *All these things the pagans seek.*
> *Your heavenly Father knows that you need them all.*
>
> Matthew 6:31–32

These are some of the things I worry about every day, Lord:

And yet, God, you tell me not to worry.
"Trust me," you say, "trust me!"
But do I really trust you?
As I think about this question right now, I would say that I

Reflection
When we place our trust in God's providence, we know
that everything will work out for the best.

My prayer:
Loving and caring God, increase my trust in you.
When I find myself worried or concerned, please

Jesus Christ is truly risen. Alleluia!

I am with you always, until the end of the age.

Matthew 28:20

Getting to know Jesus is the work of a lifetime.

Reflection
If I want to know God, I must look to Jesus.
If I want to know what God asks of me,
I need to listen to Jesus.

My prayer:
My greatest desire is to know you, God.
Hear my prayer that I

LISTEN

No one comes to the Father except through me.

John 14:6

I am in my Father and you are in me and I in you.

John 14:20

Am I listening?

My prayer:
Jesus, you want me to hear that

Behold, the kingdom of God is among you.

This is no ordinary kingdom!
It's not about palaces and guards and gold and glitter.
It's about a person.
It's about Jesus.

All-loving God, I am a member of your kingdom.
I belong to you. You are

. . . . **Journaling Notes** . . . .

Use this space for any other thoughts you might have.

Jesus Christ is truly risen. Alleluia!

...e Lord and Giver of Life

No one can say, "Jesus is Lord," except by the holy Spirit.

1 Corinthians 12:3

Holy Spirit,
Lord and Giver of Life,
you dwell in me. You are closer
to me than I could ever imagine.
Help me to come to know you
and to

Come, Holy Spirit, fill the hearts of your faithful.

Where there is a life, there is breath.
Breath is essential to life.

What a great image this is of you, Holy Spirit!
You are the Giver of Life.
You are the breath of life for us.

My prayer:
Holy Spirit, Lord and Giver of Life,
send your breath of life upon me.
Fill my heart with your Spirit so that I

> *I will ask the Father, and he will give you another Advocate*
> *to be with you always, the Spirit of truth.*
> John 14:16–17

Reflection

Holy Spirit, Lord and Giver of Life,
you are the Advocate promised by the
risen Lord to be with us and for us forever.

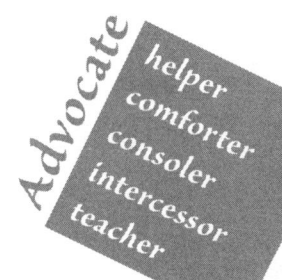

My prayer:

Holy Spirit, I know I need to become
more tuned into your presence in my life.
When I am tempted or afraid,

Pentecost

The disciples gathered together,
and tongues of fire came to rest
on them. They were filled with the Holy Spirit. They now had
the courage and strength to be your witnesses.

Fill me with your spirit, O Lord.
Let the fire of your love burn in my heart so that I

The Holy Spirit dwells in each of us.

*Do you not know that you are the temple of God,
and that the Spirit of God dwells in you?*

1 Corinthians 3:16

My Identity

I am a temple of God.
The Holy Spirit dwells in me.
I participate in the very life of God.

Is this the person I believe I am?

Holy Spirit, you know me.
You see me as I am.
Help me to

A Life of Grace ....

Holy Spirit, the wonderful thing about all this is
that you have not left me on my own.
You are with me, and your grace is with me.
I am never without the grace I need.

My prayer to the Holy Spirit:

You will receive power when the holy Spirit comes
upon you, and you will be my witnesses in Jerusalem,
throughout Judea and Samaria, and to the ends of the earth.

Acts 1:8

Holy Spirit, Lord and Giver of Life,
I am to be your witness, not in Jerusalem,
but here in my own hometown.
To be your witness, I know that I have to

.... Journaling Notes ....
Use this space for any other thoughts you might have.

The Holy Spirit dwells in each of us.

CHAPTER 11

The Mystery of the Church

> *I will take you as my own people,*
> *and you shall have me as your God.*
>
> *Exodus 6:7*

*hurch* — belonging to the Lord
— a people called together

Reflection

Belonging to the Church is not something to be taken for granted. It's something very special. It means God thought about me and chose me to be among his people. Do I think about this?

How is belonging to the Church making a difference in my life, or is it? Dear God,

> *The Church is Christ's faithful people, the people of God.*

The People of God

The people of God are ordinary people like you and me.
God works through his people.
That means God works through me! What a thought!

My prayer:

Loving God, you work through me in many ways.
Help me to

Images of The Church

When people use the expression "it's a piece of cake,"
I know what they mean. I make a connection.
Images help me to understand and make connections.

Body of Christ

The image of the Church as the body of Christ helps me
make a connection: As a member of the Church, I am
part of the body of Christ. What an awesome thought!

Dear God,
Help me to

The Family of God

What a great image this is for the Church! The Church welcomed
me into the family of God when I was baptized.

Just knowing that I belong to your family, God, helps me to

My prayer for the Family of God

45

The Church is the living body of Christ.

An Event

The Church is an **Event**.
Something happens when the people of God
come together. God is worshiped and people are served.
Now that's an event!
That's Church!

. . . .

Reflection

It is not enough for me to say I belong to the Church.
There is more to it than that.
I must be part of the worshiping community,
and I must be willing to serve others.

Where am I in all this? Am I a spectator? a missing person?
a participant in the event?

Dear God,

> *"Go, therefore, and make disciples of all nations."*
> *Matthew 28:19*

Missionaries risk their lives to make disciples of people in all
parts of the world.

How am I helping to make disciples?

Grant me, O Lord,

a deeper love and appreciation of the Church.

Grant me, O Lord, a greater desire to

. . . . Journaling Notes . . . .

Use this space for any other thoughts you might have.

The Church is the living body of Christ.

CHAPTER 12

The Church of Jesus Christ

> *I say to you, you are Peter, and upon this rock*
> *I will build my church.*
>
> *Matthew 16:18*

Roots

People care about their roots. They want to know about the beginnings of their story. Knowing our roots can make a difference in our lives.

Reflection

The roots of the Church began over two thousand years ago with Jesus and his small band of twelve apostles. How does knowing the roots of my faith make a difference in my life?

My prayer:

Jesus, your Church is alive and well today, after all these years. It's exciting for me to realize that I

Establishing A Church

Reflection

Imagine the scene in which Jesus is telling the apostles about building his Church. No blueprints, no models, no bricks and cement **—just people and a message!**
Do you think they had a clue about what he really meant?

My prayer:

Jesus, sometimes I don't have a clue about what you are telling me, but I have the Church to help me. It is always a help to me when I

The astronauts commit themselves to their space mission.
They form a team, train hard, and take off!
They know they are only a part of the space program;
other teams will follow after them.

Reflection

Peter and the other apostles committed themselves to their mission.
They formed a team, trained hard, and took off to build a Church.
They knew they were only the beginning. Others would follow
to carry on the Church.

My prayer:

Jesus, today it's my turn to carry on the mission
of the Church. This is no easy job.
I need you to

If Peter and a few of the other apostles showed up in my
parish church next Sunday, what would they think of us?

What might surprise them?

Would they find me there?

What would I want to say to them about the Church?

Christ founded his Church on the apostles.

Scripture UPDATE

If anything is clear in the gospels, it is the close relationship Christ had with his apostles. They were the foundation upon which he built the Church. Our link to Christ and his mission is through the bishops, the successors to the apostles.

Jesus put Peter in charge of the newly formed band of apostles. Jesus had given them both a mission to accomplish and the authority to carry it out. It was Peter's duty to keep them on track.

Reflection

Today the bishop is the one in charge. He is responsible for keeping the Church on track. He is the direct successor to the apostles. Without him the link to Christ through the apostles would be missing. No wonder the Church prays at every Mass for the bishop!

My prayer for the bishop of my diocese:

My prayer for the pope, the bishop of Rome:

I am a Catholic, and I belong to the Church.
Belonging to the Church is something special.

Some things I want to say about belonging to the Catholic Church are:

. . . . Journaling Notes . . . .

Use this space for any other thoughts you might have.

Christ founded his Church on the apostles.

CHAPTER 13

Catholicism: A Way of Life

> *The harvest is abundant but the laborers are few.*
>
> Luke 10:2

Reflection

Lord, I hear you loud and clear. The Church has work to be done and you need me to help, now, today! No waiting around.

The Church needs me now.
My parish needs me now.

If I really believe I'm needed, I know I will have to

There are many things I can do to serve the Church. For instance, I can

Something I especially like to do in my parish is

My prayer:
Lord Jesus,

The parish is our home
in the Catholic Church
from the first moment
of our lives to the last.

Reflection

My life in the Church began at my Baptism.
My name is officially inscribed in the parish where
I was baptized. From that day on the parish became
my home in the Church. What an amazing thing!

Home can mean many things. It can mean pitching in,
talking things over, eating together. For me it means

My parish is important to me. It helps me by

The parish can do just so much. I need to do my part.
I need to pitch in and

My prayer:

Loving God, give me a greater love for my parish and
a deeper desire to serve you.
Help me, especially,

My life in the Church began at Baptism.

Our Catholic Way of Life

> *And whatever you do, in word or in deed,*
> *do everything in the name of the Lord Jesus,*
> *giving thanks to God the Father through him.*
>
> *Colossians 3:17*

Paul is telling me that to be a member of the Church
I am to do everything in the name of the Lord Jesus.
Everything!

How can I do everything in your name, Lord?

What about my **words**? Do they give you honor?
My prayer:

And what about my **deeds**? Does what I do give you honor, Lord?
My prayer:

World Youth Day

Thousands of youth from all over the world gather together for several days to celebrate their Catholic faith. Young people of different cultures, customs, and languages, all worship and pray as one.

The pope celebrates Mass for the youth of the world. That includes me! He prays that we will live the faith and serve our Church with great love and zeal.

My prayer for the youth of the world:

. . . . Journaling Notes . . . .

Use this space for any other thoughts you might have.

My life in the Church began at Baptism.

CHAPTER 14

The Church On its Way

> Stay awake, for you know neither the day nor the hour.
>
> Matthew 25:13

Stay Awake! Stay Awake!
Christ Is Coming Again!

Reflection

Jesus is talking about more than **Not Sleeping**.
He's talking about the final countdown.
About getting everything in order.
The clock is ticking! Christ is coming again!

Jesus, if I knew when you were coming, would I stay awake?
Would I have everything in order? Would you find me among
your faithful followers?

My prayer:

Jesus, I believe that you will come again and that

> *I will see you again, and your hearts will rejoice,*
> *and no one will take your joy away from you.*
>
> John 16:22

Making Choices

God does not choose heaven or hell for any one of us; we choose it for ourselves.

Every person must make this choice. No exceptions!

Heaven – eternal happiness with God

Hell – eternal separation from God

Reflection

Choosing heaven or hell! What kind of a choice is that?
It's a choice that affects everything I will ever do. It's a choice
I must make between happiness with God and separation from God.

Dear God,
Don't let me be fooled into thinking it's no big deal,
that I can think about it tomorrow or next week.
I want to be with you, God, and that means

By the way we live now, we choose heaven or hell.

Mary, the First Disciple

Mother Of God

At the Annunciation Mary said *yes* to God's invitation.
Her *yes* brought Jesus into the world.
Her *yes* changed the world forever.

Yes

Reflection

Saying *yes* is not always easy. Sometimes my *yes*
can make the difference between right and wrong.
Sometimes my *yes* can change my life forever.

Some things I know God is asking me to say *yes* to:

My prayer:

Mary, my Mother, you are the Morning Star of my life.
You

Our beliefs give meaning to everything we do.

My God, I believe in you. You give meaning to my life.
I want to thank you especially for

. . . . Journaling Notes . . . .

Use this space for any other thoughts you might have.

By the way we live now, we choose heaven or hell.

CHAPTER 15

Bringing the World to Christ

Through faith you are all children of God in Christ Jesus.

Galatians 3:26

Jesus, you have chosen me as a member of your Church to be your evangelizer.

Jesus, you really believe in me, don't you?
You have confidence that I can be your evangelizer.
I want to live up to what you expect of me.

My prayer:

Help me to transform my own life and so be a witness to my family.

I can be a better witness to my family if I

Help me to see each day where I can bring the message of your good news to others.

I can bring the good news to others today when I

*Young people who are well trained
in faith and prayer must become
more and more the apostles of youth.
The Church counts greatly on their contribution.*

Pope Paul VI. On Evangelization, 72

Jesus, I have tried to be an evangelizer to my family and friends.
I remember a time when I really did reach out to others.

My story of being an evangelizer

Evangelization: bringing the good news to the world.

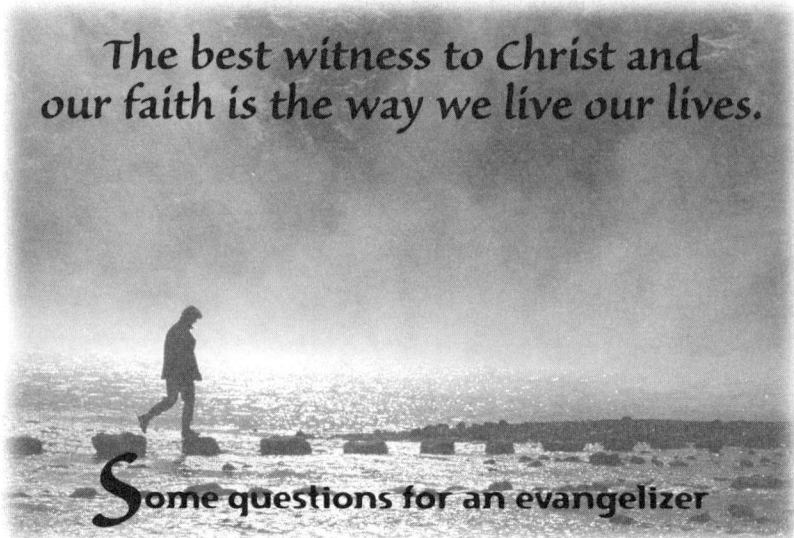

The best witness to Christ and our faith is the way we live our lives.

Some questions for an evangelizer

Will I persevere in resisting evil and, whenever I fall into sin, repent and return to the Lord?

With your help, God, I will do this by

Will I proclaim by word and example the good news of God in Christ?

With your help, God, I will do this by

Will I seek and serve Christ in all persons?

With your help, God, I will do this by

*The Church has so much to talk about
with youth, and youth have so much
to talk about with the Church.*

Pope John Paul II
The Lay Faithful, 46

If I could talk to the Holy Father today here are some things
I would share with him about the Church:

. . . . Journaling Notes . . . .

Use this space for any other thoughts you might have.

Evangelization: bringing the good news to the world.

Acknowledgments

Scripture selections taken from the *New American Bible* Copyright © 1991, 1986, 1970 Confraternity of Christian Doctrine, Washington, D.C. and are used by license of the copyright owner. All rights reserved. No part of the *New American Bible* may be used or reproduced in any form, without permission in writing from the copyright owner.

The English translation of the Apostles' Creed by the International Consultation on English Texts (ICET).

Photo Credits

Photo Editor
Jim Saylor

Associate Photo Editor
Lori Berkowitz

Adventure Photo and Film: 14; Pressenbild: 13; Steven Alvarez: 17; Michael Powers: 38.
CLEO Photography: 30.
Comstock: 33.
Crosiers/Gene Plaisted, OSC: back cover, top front cover, 10.
FPG/Andrea Sperling: 16; Toyohiro Yamada: 52.
Robert Fried: 26.
Gamma Liaison Network/F. Lo Chan: 6.
Anne Hamersky: 20.
Bob Hand: 22.
Image Bank/Grant V. Faint: 58; Alexander Stewart: 62.
Richard Pasley: 18.
Sygma/G. Giansanti: 55.
Tony Stone Images: 34; Hugh Sitton: 5; Richard Passmore: 28.
Larry Ulrich: 36.
Uniphoto: 40.
Viesti: 8.
Leo de Wys/Riclafe: 61.